LETTER WRITING

Jackie Elton

THE INDUSTRIAL SOCIETY

First published in 1979 by
The Industrial Society
48 Bryanston Square
London W1H 7LN
Telephone: 071-262 2401

Reprinted (10th) 1992

© *The Industrial Society 1979*

ISBN 0 85290 389 8

All rights reserved. No part of this publication may be reproduced, stored in a retrieval system or transmitted, in any form or by any means, electronic, mechanical, photocopying, recording and/or otherwise without the prior written permission of the publishers. This book may not be lent, resold, hired out or otherwise disposed of by way of trade in any form, binding or cover other than that in which it is published, without prior consent of the publisher.

CONTENTS

Foreword

1 Introduction	1
2 Planning	2
Why?	2
Who?	2
How?	3
When?	4
What?	4
3 Structuring	5
Greeting	5
Introduction	5
Facts	7
Action	7
Concluding remarks	8
4 Writing	9
Accuracy	9
Brevity	10
Clarity	12
Tone	13
5 Checking	16
6 Working effectively with a Secretary	17
7 Dealing with different types of letters	19
Complaints	19
Getting Action	20
Selling	21
8 Punctuation	22
9 Layout	24

Appendix 1 - **Examples**   25

Appendix 2 - **Further Reading**   32

Appendix 3 - **Industrial Society courses**   33

FOREWORD

The ability to write clear, informative letters is an essential part of working life. It is a skill required at many levels in an organisation and is an integral part of the whole process of communication.

Writing accurate, structured letters which achieve results is not a mysterious talent. It can be learnt by following some basic ground rules and guidelines. The Industrial Society has produced this book to help people acquire the necessary skills.

Jacqueline Elton's book provides a step by step guide to successful, effective letter writing.

YVONNE BENNION
Division Director

1 INTRODUCTION

Letter writing is a skill which requires a blend of common sense, patience and an understanding of people. It does not require a voluminous vocabulary and total familiarity with every aspect of syntax and grammar.

It is essential that letters we send out are of a high standard. They need to communicate to the reader. That means:

"Create understanding in the minds of others and get action."

This guide will look at the three key steps you need to take to get letters right.

- Planning
- Writing and Structuring
- Checking that the letter meets the writer's and reader's needs.

Many people would say that style should be individual. This is true. It is very difficult to write to set formats as letters go out of date very quickly and sound impersonal to the reader.

On the other hand, a good writing style must primarily be designed to help the reader understand and act. In the end, the good letter is read and the bad letter gathers dust in the tray or even the waste-paper basket. In all organisations, we judge our writing by the results achieved.

2 PLANNING

Even a short letter needs to be planned in advance. The extra thought before putting pen to paper is likely to help save your time in writing and the reader's time in reading. It will also ensure you achieve the objective of the letter.

Why?

It is easy when writing the routine letter to forget precisely what your purpose is. Letters are normally written for one or more of the following reasons:

- To give information and ideas
- To get a specific action or series of actions
- To persuade or sell
- To put a situation right - perhaps restoring a relationship with a customer
- To clarify a situation
- To create a good impression of ourselves and our organisation.

Most letters contain one or more of these objectives. Be very clear which is the most important. If you do not have a precise understanding of what you want to achieve, then you will fail and the reader will not understand your letter.

All business letters should create a good impression (objective 6), even if there is a conflict with the reader.

It is also worth asking: Why write a letter? Perhaps a telephone call would be better in that it can provide instant feedback. A letter, on the other hand, can provide clear details and can be kept as a record.

Who?

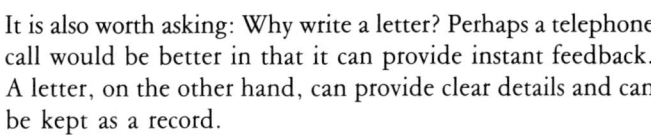

To whom are you writing? It helps to know as much about the reader as possible.

If you are writing to people whom you have never met, you should still be able to build up a picture of them. You should find out:

- How much they know about you and the situation.

- What is their level of understanding? ie jargon, technical knowledge. It is usually much better to pitch a little lower rather than too high. Provided your tone is not patronising, the reader will rarely be insulted by use of simple words and explanations.
- Their attitudes and feelings towards your organisation.
- Their objectives. What do they want? These will not always be the same as yours.
- Their authority. Are they in a position to respond? Age and status will help you to decide how to write. If in doubt, think of somebody you know well who might resemble the reader and adopt the tone you think most suitable.

How?

We will look at writing style in the next chapter. It is important to think about how you want the letter to sound. It is closely related to the purpose and who you are writing to.

Letters used to be very formal. Styles have now changed, become far less formal and closer to the way we would speak. If the image of your organisation is to be friendly, professional, caring, reassuring and efficient, then that must be reflected in the tone of the letter. It is worth looking at the letters we receive and thinking about the image that they present.

We all have individual styles which reflect our background and personality. It is also important to think not just how we like to express things but how our readers would like to see them expressed. That is the test of good communication.

When?

Letters often take longer to write than we think. There is time for writing, typing, checking and ending. Be realistic about this. Leave time if necessary to rewrite it if you feel the end product is unlikely to achieve its objective. It is also important to take the reader's timetable into account. When are they most likely to read it? How quickly can they respond?

What?

After getting the answer to the above questions, you can then decide what to write. Collect relevant facts, details, names, dates, past history and check them. Then make a list of the RELEVANT items and put them in sequence.

A very simple method is to do a pattern plan or spider diagram.

Example

Imagine you are writing to a theatre to book some tickets. Telephone bookings are not accepted. You have to ensure all the details are correct.

- Take a plain sheet of paper and write the subject in the centre.
- Write down all the ideas and thoughts you have branching out along the lines of connected ideas.
- Then eliminate any irrelevant points and put it in a sequence that would suit the reader.

Making a plan is a very quick process and a safeguard against leaving out crucial information. The shorter the letter, the quicker it will be to plan and organise. With long letters, it will be necessary to put the different points under larger headings and numbered paragraphs.

3 STRUCTURING

Every business letter needs a structure; it saves time and confusion. It helps the reader to understand the letter and take the necessary action without having to re-read it. Almost all letters can be structured in the following order:

- Greeting
- Introduction
- Facts
- Action
- Concluding remarks.

Greeting

Dear Sir/Madam

We should use this form only if we do not know what the reader is called and have no way of finding out.

Using people's names is professional, friendly and much more likely to get a response. If you receive a letter addressed to you personally, you are more likely to feel committed to responding.

Dear Mr/Mrs/Miss/Ms

In most cases, it is best to use one of these alternatives. Deciding to write to "Dear Fred" or "Dear Christine" depends on your own level of contact and the attitudes of the people to whom you are writing. Lawyers will expect greater formality than people in advertising.

Ms

Many people worry about how to address a professional woman where they are unsure of marital status.

Some women put their title after the signature to clarify any misunderstanding. The majority do not. In that case, Ms is quite acceptable to the majority of women in business. Using Ms saves time, worry and having to make an assumption which could be a mistake and cause offence. If in doubt, telephone the company and find out.

Introduction

The first paragraph of a letter should immediately and clearly identify:

The subject matter of the letter

If you are answering a request - do not simply put "as requested" - state what the request actually is.

The date

Always refer to the date of their letter so they can check their file. It is also very important if, in the future, there is a need to identify a clear chronological order of events.

If they have not put a date, never refer to their undated letter. Instead refer to the date the letter was received. Otherwise, you are drawing attention to their lack of professionalism.

Heading

Almost all letters benefit from a clear heading. It looks professional and acts like a newspaper headline. It focuses the reader's attention on the subject. Try to ensure the heading is meaningful to the reader, not just to you. For example, heading a letter "Order No. 3379" may mean very little to a reader while "Installation of Shower Unit" will be more helpful.

Replying to a letter

There are several ways of replying:

- "Thank you for your letter dated 20th January 1991."

This is the easiest and most straightforward method. Not only is it concise but it is also polite. Even if the letter you have received is not friendly, even a complaint, it is still constructive to thank the person for taking the trouble to write.

- "With reference to your letter dated 20th January 1991 we have investigated the problem and found that...."

The difficulty with starting in this way is that you cannot put a full stop after the date. This would create an incorrect sentence and you would have to allow the flow to continue. This will mean a long sentence and jumping too quickly into the main facts of the letter.

- "I refer to your letter of 20th January 1991."

This is quite acceptable but rather formal.

Initiating a contact

Refer clearly to the event which prompted you to write:

- I saw your advertisement in last Tuesday's *Evening Post*.
- I understand from Jeffrey Taylor that your company is interested in....
- We met at the recent opening of the Wilkinson factory.

Remember: first impressions do count.

Facts

This is the meat of the letter. As part of the preparation you will have the relevant facts sorted out into logical order on a sheet of paper. Make sure these are accurate and complete. If there is very much information, use paragraphs and give each paragraph a heading. If necessary, number the paragraphs.

eg: Dear Miss Wilson

Conditions of Employment

We would like to offer you the position of Complaints Clerk in our London office, subject to the following conditions:

Pay

Your salary will be x per annum, paid monthly in arrears by credit transfer.

Pension scheme

The company operates a contributory pension scheme which you will be required to join....

Action

Finally you will need to make sure that your letter indicates:

- What action needs to be taken.
- When it is to be taken - deadlines should be as specific as possible.
- Who is expected to take it.

This paragraph of the letter should be clearly distinguishable from the features or facts - so that it stands out. Be careful not to be too abrupt or demanding in the way you ask for action. Also it is important to be realistic. Never promise or ask for the moon. Actions should be specific and achievable.

Concluding remarks

If you leave the letter at the Action stage, it sounds rather abrupt. The last line of the letter should provide the polite and human touch.

Example

"I look forward to hearing from you."

"I hope this information will be useful."

"Thank you for your help with this project. I enjoyed meeting you and look forward to working with you again in the future."

Remember that this part of the letter is personal. It is essential not to sign off with very standard and stale statements.

Example

"Assuring you of our best attention at all times."

"Please do not hesitate to contact me."

These are used so often that they sound too much like a cliche and lack of personal touch. Find something which sounds natural. Think about what you would say face to face and then put it into an acceptable form.

4 WRITING

Once you have a clear purpose and structure, the writing itself becomes much easier. We all have personal style but this does not mean we should avoid the basic rules of good business writing. This is the ABC of writing:

- Accurate
- Brief
- Clear

Your key aim is to help the reader to understand. It is not to impress nor to battle. You should want to write the letter that the reader finds easy to read, simple and straightforward.

Accuracy

Facts should be correct, complete and relevant. In other words: the truth, the whole truth and nothing but the truth.

Do your best to make sure that the picture you have in your mind is the one which ends up in the reader's mind. Accuracy depends on accurate facts.

If the facts are a blur, the spellings and names not checked, the meaning will be lost.

It can be important to be specific, eg rather than saying "Later" we should say "two hours later".

Avoid making the assumption that the reader is as aware of the facts as you are. Check that the phrases are not ambiguous.

Example

"If you think goods are unsatisfactory you should see our manager."

In general make sure that information in a letter sets out the necessary background, time factors, numbers, exact location and people involved.

Accurate Words

Some words mean different things to different people.

Before the miners' srike in 1984 there was an agreement that "economic" coal mines would not be closed. The trouble started when all sides showed they had totally different ideas of what the word "economic" meant. Even quite common words that we use and think we understand may mean something else to someone else.

The correct meaning of "feasible" is "practicable" but many people have defined it as "probable", "plausible" or even "possible but unlikely".

Often the best we can do is to use a simple word that is instantly recognisable to the reader — usually short and used regularly in speech.

Watch words which get confused through similar spellings.

Example

Council	an assembly
Counsel	advise
Complement	that which completes
Compliment	praise

Brevity

In other words, keep it short.

Bernard Shaw once wrote a very long letter to a friend. He apologised saying "I didn't have the time to write you a shorter one."

If you keep it short, you save the reader's time. It may mean, however, that you have to spend longer planning. It is quite easy to write pages without carefully selecting what it is the reader needs or wants to know.

We should write the minimum necessary to achieve the purpose of the letter.

Short Sentences

The shorter a sentence, the easier it is to understand.

4% of readers will understand a 27 word sentence at first reading.

75% of readers will understand a 17 word sentence at first reading.

95% of readers will understand an 8 word sentence at first reading.

If sentences are kept below 20 words, their impact will be much greater. If a sentence is to have a very strong impact, it should be less than 10 words long, for instance, at the beginning of a letter or paragraph.

Short Words

Never use a long word where a short one will do. The effect will be sharper, clearer and more easy to read.

Long Word	Short Word
Request	Ask
Require	Need
Proceed	Go ahead
Materialise	Happen
Terminate	End
Despatch	Send
Purchase	Buy

Sometimes there are important reasons for using longer words. They may have useful overtones or simply express a feeling more appropriately. As a rule, however, short words have more impact and communicate better than long words.

Short Phrases

So many letters could be better if only we learnt to abandon wordy phrases that, for some reason, we have become attached to. It may be we have picked them up from other people or that we have just got into the habit. Very often we could drop entire phrases or cut them down to one or two words:

Phrase	Short form
Please do not hesitiate to	Please
At this moment in time	Now
In the normal course of our procedure	Normally
In the event of	If
Endeavour to ascertain	Try to find out
We have discontinued the policy of	We no longer
We are of the opinion that	We think/believe
We have pleasure in enclosing herewith	We enclose

"It" constructions can sound heavy, eg:

It was noted that if	If
It was suggested by Mr X	Mr X suggested

Clarity

Clear writing does for a reader what a clear day does for a driver. In means quick, efficient reading without having to stop and check obstacles along the way. The opposite of clear is dull, obscure, cloudy, foggy.

Make yourself clear:

- Start by making the subject and purpose clear, ie give a proper introduction.
- Check the progression is logical, ie give a structure.
- Use the active, not passive voice.

Example

Passive: The contents of the flat were examined.
Active: The police examined the contents of the flat.

Passive: It was decided in the meeting that....
Active: The meeting decided....

The active is much easier to understand and provides more impact.

- Be precise, avoid vague phrases such as 'in the region of', 'in the area of' or 'around about'.
- Imagine explaining the facts orally to the reader.
- Use headings and consistent numbering.
- Use jargon only in its rightful place.

In many fields we have to use terminology to express the ideas and methods involved. There is also "in house" jargon used by a group of people or a company.

Always check your assumption that the reader will understand the jargon used. Look for simple words or even analogies which will help the reader to understand.

- Watch the use of abbreviations, initials and Latin words.

Abbreviations are very often not understood or

Ipso facto, we have not found your umbrella per se, but we will search ad infinitum.

confused. Latin words create a psychological barrier in readers who lack confidence in their knowledge and education.

Tone

Once the language used in a letter is clear and easy to follow, it will also be essential to consider the tone.

Each letter you send is an ambassador for yourself and the organisation for which you work.

Consider what the letter is supposed to achieve. Getting action from the reader may require facts and a conciliatory manner - or perhaps a more assertive tone. Think about the impact your choice of words will have.

Be positive not negative

Avoid, where possible, using negative sounding words or phrases. Look for positive alternatives.

Example

Negative: We are unable to reserve a room until 15th September.

Positive: We can reserve you a room at any time after 14th September.

Sound definite

This does not mean promising what you cannot deliver. It is about avoiding uncertain words and hedging unnecessarily.

Words like "I will try", "perhaps", "may" will not inspire a reader's confidence. It is important that you check your facts and options and set them down with assurance.

Example

We will try to deliver the goods to you by Monday.

The goods will be delivered to you Monday 10.00 am if the traffic situation is clear.

Emotive Words

It is sometimes necessary to avoid words that a reader might feel to be a personal attack on them or their organisation.

Example

Bad	• Your failure to reply
Good	• I have not received a reply
Bad	• Your refusal to cooperate
Good	• As you feel we should not continue to work jointly
Bad	• Your unreasonable attitude
Good	• As we clearly disagree
Bad	• You have not understood
Good	• There seems to be a misunderstanding

Remember to state the facts as you and the reader might see them. Choose words that will help you to achieve your objectives. Sometimes you can feel angry, frustrated or simply impatient with a person or situation. This feeling will pass but if you vent your feelings in a letter the effects may be, in the long term, very serious.

Imperatives

If you write a letter to get action, beware of being too "bossy".

Example

Bad — Your interview has been arranged for Thursday at 3.00 pm.

Good — We would like you to attend an interview on Thursday at 3.00 pm.

Formality

Letters have become far less formal over the years. We rarely see phrases now like:

"I remain, sir, your obedient servant"

Few people are impressed by formality and often it can create barriers. The trend is definitely in the direction of "writing as you speak" and plain English. This does not mean sloppy language, slang or over familiarity.

Remember your reader is a human being who appreciates openness and friendliness and can react to the wrong word used in the wrong place.

5 CHECKING

Letters should be checked before they reach the typist and on their return. Most people simply check spellings, punctuation and other obvious errors. This is not enough. Think about all aspects of the letter. Here is a checklist.

Ask yourself:

- Does this letter present a good image of the company?
- Does it look interesting and easy to read? Is the layout right?
- Does your purpose come over clearly?
- Are all the facts there? Are they in the right order?
- Does it say what you meant to say?
- Is the tone right?
- Is it clear who should do what, next?
- Is it the right length? Check the paragraphs, phrases, words and sentences.
- Is the language easy to understand? Free from jargon?
- Have you got copies for everyone who needs to know about the letter?

6 WORKING EFFECTIVELY WITH A SECRETARY

No matter how carefully you have prepared and composed your letter, it will all be wasted unless the end product is a good one.

Whether you have your own secretary or your letters are dealt with by the typing pool, you should try to work as a team with your typist. You must agree on the layout for your letters and discuss any other relevant points so that your terms of reference are quite clear. Remember to follow "house style" if there is one. Typing other people's letters can be a tedious task so if the writer takes the time to involve the typist, the benefits will show in the work.

Dictating

If you dictate your letters rather than draft them in longhand, always try to book sufficient time with the secretary so that you can avoid piecemeal dictation.

Pre-plan your letter as if you were going to write it out so that your dictation will follow a logical structure. Give the secretary all the relevant papers, and dictate rhythmically. Remember, most types of shorthand are written in phrases, not individual words.

Audio Dictation

When dictating into a machine, try and think as a secretary who is about to type what you are saying. It is easy when taking shorthand to ask for information to be repeated or clarified.

Try to anticipate problem areas for the typist. Always pre-plan the letter, and dictate rhythmically. Try to find as quiet a place as possible. Make sure the typist can hear your instructions and not the rumble of the train.

Check after a few words that the tape is recording properly. Give the typist instructions about the number of copies required before you dictate the letter. Remember the typist hears, then types at once.

Give the punctuation as you go along. It is difficult for the typist to sense the structure of a sentence when audio typing. Spell ambiguous or difficult words and names.

7 DEALING WITH DIFFERENT TYPES OF LETTERS

Some letters need particularly sensitive handling. Here are some guidelines on the approach to:

- Dealing with letters of complaint
- Getting action
- Selling

Complaints

Nobody wants to receive a letter of complaint. The fact is that, in almost any organisation, they will be received unless we are perfect. The natural reaction is to get upset and defensive. The professional approach is to treat a complaint as an opportunity. Most people do not bother to complain. They simply go elsewhere and perhaps tell their acquaintances not to use your organisation.

Those who complain are taking the time and effort to point out what has happened and how they feel about it. Your purpose in writing a letter back is to put things right and try to restore the relationship with the person concerned.

Your response to a complaint naturally depends on the situation. Guidelines are set out below for each case. Note that all three start by thanking the reader for their letter and expressing sympathy.

We are wrong and must admit it

- Thank you for your letter
- I am sorry
- Explain what happened - not in detail
- Say what will be done, when and how
- Yours sincerely

We are right but in the interests of public relations meet the claim

- Thank you for your letter
- Sympathise, show concern
- Say what we are prepared to do
- Explain how to prevent the same thing happening again
- Yours sincerely

We are right and are not prepared to meet the claim

- Thank you for your letter
- Sympathise
- I can understand your point
- However, this is our point
- Because of our point we can't help
- Explain how to prevent a similar occurrence in future
- Yours sincerely

Getting Action

When you have been let down, fobbed off with excuses, debts are unpaid, goods undelivered, a letter can be crucial. Extra care should be taken to plan a letter of action.

Why?

What, precisely, do you want to achieve? What actions, who by and what dates? What can you realistically expect to achieve? What compromises would you accept?

Who?

Who should you write to? On the whole it should be the person who can do the action - or in some circumstances that person's superior. To write higher up or through an indirect route may be effective but may also create a strong antagonism and a greater defensiveness.

What?

Keep to the structure outlined in Chapter 3. Make sure you state your facts first and provide evidence. Dates, names and times are very effective in making your case.

Avoid subjective comments and emotive language which invite dispute. Show that you are reasonable and have material to support your point of view.

Action

Outline the action and deadlines you are looking for from them. Give them a deadline which gives enough time and after which you can write again. If necessary, put in sanctions that they would appreciate. Empty threats will put you in a weak position.

Selling

A sales letter should:

Gain the reader's interest
Create belief in your service
Get action and sales

- Address the letters only to people who have the authority and need to buy. Use their names - it prompts a greater response. Form a mental picture of them and their needs. Build the letter round them, not yourself.

- Describe the benefits not the features of your service. For example, electric windows on a car are a feature; convenience and comfort are the benefits. What benefit or combination is most likely to affect your readers? Is there anything topical or new about the service that would provide extra appeal?

- Use words that appeal positively:

    | need | security | best |
    | exceptional | benefits | discount |
    | value | guaranteed | new |

- Avoid "hype" that creates scepticism:

    | fantastic | totally unique | fabulous |

- Make the letter easy to answer. Set out clear actions and deadlines to guide the reader. If possible, provide an added incentive to encourage an early reply.

8 PUNCTUATION

Punctuation does for the written word what pauses do for speech. It is there to help the reader understand. People sometimes worry about what punctuation to use. If you are uncertain about when to punctuate, write short sentences less than twenty words long.

Here is a brief list of some punctuation marks and rules. If you would like a more thorough list, please refer to Appendix 3.

Commas

Commas are a way of separating nouns, phrases, adjectives and clauses from each other. Be careful not to put too many in - it can make the reader gasp rather than breathe.

Example

"The room was filled with chairs, tables, teacups and stationery."

"The children went fishing, played football, drank orange squash and ate ice cream."

Semi-colon

This is a longer pause, about half way between a comma and a full stop. It separates two clauses which are closely linked but could stand as sentences on their own.

Example

"The sales presentation was a great success; it exceeded our wildest hopes."

Colon

The colon introduces a list.

Example

"I met several people that day: soldiers, sailors, businessmen, villagers and fishermen."

When the colon introduces a list of clauses, the points can be separated by semi-colons instead of commas as above.

Example

"She watched people in the park: some rushed past; others ambled slowly; still more sat and enjoyed the sunshine."

Apostrophe

This shows possession.

Example

"The cat's whiskers." (singular)
"The boys' pens."(plural)

It can also be in place of an omitted letter.

Example

"I don't want to see you." instead of "I do not want to see you."

9 LAYOUT

There are several different styles of layout for business correspondence. The most common styles are "indented", eg:

  12 Milton Crescent
    Winchester
      Hampshire

  Dear Sirs
    I have received...

and "block", eg

    12 Milton Crescent
    Winchester
    Hampshire

    Dear Sirs
    I have received...

The same style follows right through the letter. Your company may have a preferred style of layout. The important thing, once you have decided which to use, is to be consistent.

The presentation of your letter will often mean success or failure in achieving its purpose. Remember that each letter takes its chance among a volume of other correspondence on the average desk. It will greatly help if it is well presented and easy to read.

Think about the psychological effect on the reader. Short paragraphs, spaces, headings and numbering make the letter inviting to read.

Which would most readers prefer to read?

APPENDIX 1
EXAMPLES

Letter to the Managing Director of an organisation which is a potential customer of "ABC Company", to introduce their services.

Dear Mr Jardine

I see from recent advertisements in "Training World" that your company runs management seminars.

ABC Company has two separate suites of conference and syndicate rooms available for hire. I believe that they would be very suitable venues for your courses and meetings. I enclose a copy of our brochure which contains further information and details of our very competitive rates.

We can provide catering services and have experienced staff available to operate projectors and CCTV equipment if required.

May I suggest that you, or one of your staff, come and have a look at our facilities? I will telephone you on Monday to arrange this.

I look forward to doing business with you.

Yours sincerely

Letter from Customer Services Manager to a dissatisfied customer offering compensation.

Dear Mrs Walker

Thank you for your letter of 6 July, returning the children's jeans bought from our Slough store.

I am very sorry for the fault, which is clearly unsatisfactory.

In the circumstances, we are enclosing gift tokens to the value of £14, to cover the purchase price and to include the postage.

Thank you for taking the trouble to write to us and we are sorry once again for the inconvenience you have been caused.

Yours sincerely

Letter to a parent moving to a new borough, in answer to an enquiry about nursery facilities.

Dear Ms Lesley

Thank you for your letter of 13 July asking for information about nursery and child care facilities in our borough.

I enclose some leaflets which give details and addresses of the various centres available. The best thing is to contact the centres directly.

I hope you are able to find a suitable playschool or nursery for your child. However, do please telephone me if you need any further help.

Good luck with your move.

Yours sincerely

Letter from Group Sales Manager to guest speaker at a conference.

Dear Elizabeth

Sales Conference

Thank you so much for coming to York last week to speak to our sales managers.

Your presentation was just the right blend of hard facts and humour and was very much appreciated.

I had a meeting yesterday with my team to discuss the conference. I am sure you will be pleased to hear that we intend to implement many of the points you raised.

I am enclosing a cheque to cover your expenses and hope that we will be able to call on your expertise again.

Good luck with your own conference next month.

Very best wishes.

Yours sincerely

Letter to a hotel confirming a provisional reservation.

Dear Ms Miles

Thank you for showing me round Palmer Lodge and for the excellent lunch. Now that I have seen the facilities I would like to confirm our provisional booking for our management seminar:

Dates and Times

Sunday 12 October	16.00 hrs
to	
Friday 17 October	17.00 hrs

Seminar Facilities

Room — The Connaught suite available throughout. Chairs and tables set out in cabaret style: 4 round tables each seating 5 people, plus a table and chairs for 2 speakers.

Equipment
— Overhead projector and screen.
— Flipchart and paper.
— VHS video player and monitor.

Refreshments
— Tea and coffee to be brought into the Connaught Suite.
— Buffet lunch and table d'hote dinner menu in the restaurant (please see attached programme for break and meal times).
— We would also like tea and coffee available on arrival.

Bedrooms
— 20 single rooms with bath or shower for 5 nights: Sunday 12 October to Thursday 16 October incl.
— 2 single rooms with bath or shower for 7 nights: Saturday 11 October to Friday 17 October.

— I will send you a list of names a week before the Seminar.

I very much enjoyed meeting you; thank you for all your help.

Yours sincerely

Letter from Customer Services Manager to a dissatisfied customer.

Dear Mrs Conway

Thank you for your letter of 6 June.

I am sorry that the service you received in our Southend store was not wholly satisfactory. I appreciate your bringing this to my attention.

I have discussed the matter with Mr Greene, the Store Manager, who has now spoken to the sales assistant in question.

I do agree that caring for our customers is of prime importance. You will therefore be interested to know that we will be carrying out Customer Care training throughout the organisation, starting next Monday.

We look forward to welcoming you in our stores in the future.

Yours sincerely

Letter from a manufacturer's agent to the buyer from one of their customers.

Dear Miss Timpson

Order No. M381270

Thank you for your order, dated 12 October, for one dozen XYZ machines.

Unfortunately, we no longer stock these machines. Both we and many of our customers have found this to be an uneconomical line. However, there are alternatives on the market which we consider to be superior.

I have asked John Stamp, our new representative in your area, to telephone you this week. He will be pleased to show you these other machines and take your revised order.

I do hope that they will prove satisfactory.

Yours sincerely

Memorandum from an engineer to a colleague updating him on a project.

Memorandum

To: JMB/Bristol office   Date: 12 April
From: FRS/Head office

Subject: Sewage Treatment Works, Lower Picton.

Further to our meeting last week, I have now obtained plans and specifications from the Water Authority, which are attached.

I still have to speak to Bill Simmons at the Council to arrange a meeting with him and Bob Powell at the WA to discuss Stage II. I expect to know the date by the end of the week and will ring you on Friday at 3 pm to let you know what is happening.

Letter in response to a complaint.

Dear Miss Perkins

Thank you for your letter of 10th May. We are so sorry to hear of your accident and appreciate the difficulties this must have caused you.

We have thoroughly investigated the incident and find that we have no record of any accident at the time you mention. Our entrance guards man the reception area 24 hours a day and any accidents are fully recorded in our accident book. In bad weather, the hospital steps are gritted three times a day and kept completely free of ice. We cannot therefore accept any responsibility for your accident.

However, we do suggest that, if in future you should have any accident on our hospital grounds, you should report it immediately and seek medical attention. We will be only too happy to help you.

Thank you once again for writing; we hope that you will soon be fully recovered and back to work.

Yours sincerely

Letter to the organisers of a national business exhibition.

Dear Mr Weeks

I attended the meeting that your colleague, Ron Jones, organised last week. He suggested that I should contact you about the national exhibition you are running in February.

As you know, my company manufactures Grunge Flammets. Following my conversation with Ron, I understand that you might be interested in the possibility of setting up a stand at the exhibition to show this sort of thing.

I am out of the country on business until the 25th of this month, but will contact you as soon as I return to arrange a meeting.

I look forward to speaking to you then.

Yours sincerely

1st Letter asking for payment of a debt.

To: Chief Accountant

Dear Mr Brown

Delivery No. B-9130

We see from our accounts that you have not paid the balance for the above consignment since the first payment on 6th March 1990. This is now three months ago and we have sent you two invoices in this time:

> invoice B-9680 on 6th April for £1094.90
> invoice B-1040 on 6th May for £1094.90

The balance now due is for £2189.80 and a final invoice for this total amount is enclosed.

We realise that sometimes payments are delayed but would appreciate your settling the account by the end of this month.

Do please contact us if you have any queries or need further information.

Yours sincerely

2nd letter asking for payment.

Dear Mr Brown

Delivery No. B-9130

We wrote to you on the 5th June enclosing our final invoice for the above delivery; amount outstanding: £2189.80, invoice number: B-1140-91. Two months have now passed since that letter and we have not heard from you.

It is six months since you received our consignment to you and payment is well overdue. Our invoices state that payment should be made within 21 days of receipt of goods.

Please can you settle this account by the end of this week. We do not wish to take legal action, but if we have not received payment by then, we will be forced to contact our solicitor.

We look forward to hearing from you.

Yours sincerely

APPENDIX 2
FURTHER READING

Essay and letter writing
L G Alexander, John Murray

Roget's Thesaurus
Penguin

The Penguin English Dictionary

Training for communication
John Adair, Gower Press

Report writing
The Industrial Society

Rapid reading
The Industrial Society

Working with a secretary, a manager's guide
The Industrial Society

Working with management, a secretary's guide
The Industrial Society

Get it right
Michael Temple, John Murray
(Contains a guide to punctuation, spelling, common faults and summarising)

The complete letter writer
Greville Janner

APPENDIX 3
INDUSTRIAL SOCIETY COURSES

The Industrial Society runs a number of courses on the skills of communicating, including writing. As well as being run as public courses, they are also available as in-company courses.

Titles include:

Report writing
Letter writing
Communication skills at work
Minutes and agendas
Meetings: chairing and participating
Rapid and effective reading
Speaking in management
Speaking to groups
Interviewing - the practical skills
Interviewing - the selection techniques

For further details of any of these, contact the Communication Skills Department, Peter Runge House, 3 Carlton House Terrace, London SW1Y 5DG. Telephone 071-839 4300.